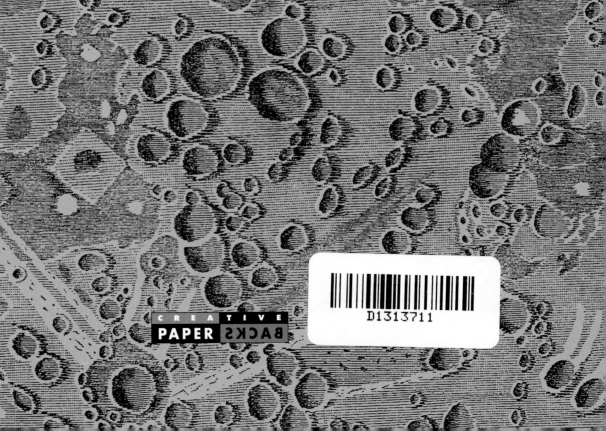

TO THE
MOON

by VALERIE BODDEN

CREATIVE
PAPER BACKS

PUBLISHED BY Creative Paperbacks
P.O. Box 227, Mankato, Minnesota 56002
Creative Paperbacks is an imprint of The Creative Company
www.thecreativecompany.us

DESIGN AND PRODUCTION BY Ellen Huber
ART DIRECTION BY Rita Marshall
PRINTED BY Corporate Graphics
in the United States of America

PHOTOGRAPHS BY
Alamy (Art Directors & TRIP, INTERFOTO), Corbis (Bettmann),
Dreamstime (Masi Gianluca), Getty Images (Apic, Ralph Morse/Time & Life Pictures,
NASA/Newsmakers, NASA/Time & Life Pictures, Rolls Press/Popperfoto, SSPL,
Space Frontiers/Hulton Archive, World Perspectives), The Granger Collection, NYC,
iStockphoto (Mike Bentley, Brandon Laufenberg), NASA

THE LIBRARY OF CONGRESS HAS CATALOGED THE HARDCOVER EDITION AS FOLLOWS:
Bodden, Valerie.
To the moon / by Valerie Bodden.
p. cm. — (Great expeditions)
Includes bibliographical references and index.
*Summary: A history of America's famed Apollo 11 mission to the moon in 1969,
detailing the challenges encountered, the individuals involved, the discoveries made,
and how the expedition left its mark upon the world.*

ISBN 978-1-60818-068-4 (hardcover)
ISBN 978-0-89812-666-2 (pbk)
1. Project Apollo (U.S.)—History—Juvenile literature. 2. Space flight to the moon—
History—Juvenile literature. I. Title.

TL789.8.U6A52195 2011
629.45'4—dc22   2010033549
CPSIA: 110310 PO1383

First Edition
2 4 6 8 9 7 5 3 1

Table of Contents

THE RACE FOR SPACE

THROUGHOUT HISTORY, HUMAN BEINGS HAVE GAZED ON THE STARS, BUT IN THE MID-20TH CENTURY, PEOPLE BEGAN TO REACH FOR THEM—LITERALLY. DURING THE 1950S AND '60S, SCIENTISTS IN BOTH THE UNITED STATES AND THE SOVIET UNION WORKED TO DEVELOP WAYS TO LAUNCH MEN INTO THE HEAVENS AND EVENTUALLY TO THE MOON. IN 1969, THIS GOAL WAS FINALLY

achieved when American astronauts Neil Armstrong and Edwin "Buzz" Aldrin of the Apollo 11 lunar mission became the first human beings to walk on the moon. Their steps forever changed the way humankind looked at Earth's SATELLITE.

Centuries before Apollo 11 rocketed to the moon, though, people had looked to that heavenly body in wonder and admiration. Many cultures worshiped lunar gods or developed myths about figures such as the man in the moon. People the world over used the moon's PHASES as a calendar, and some cultures created MEGALITHS that may have served to record or predict the moon's orbital pattern.

Apollo 11's advanced modules and rockets were constructed at facilities throughout Southern California and locations around the country.

Yet, for hundreds of years, people could only guess what the surface of the moon might look like. Around 1600, British scientist William Gilbert drew a map of the moon based on observations made with the naked eye. The map depicted Earth's satellite as being much like Earth itself, with continents surrounded by oceans. Less than a decade later, the invention of the telescope aided humankind's ability to see the features of the moon. In 1610, Italian scientist Galileo Galilei published drawings of the moon as seen through a telescope. His sketches revealed a surface covered with craters and mountains. Although Galileo did not see any water, he believed that any oceans on the moon would appear as darker areas. As a result, the moon's dark areas were later given the name "maria," Latin for "seas." (The maria are now known to be lunar plains.) As telescopes continued to improve, ASTRONOMERS published new maps; by the late 1800s, lunar maps highlighted 33,000 different physical features.

Questions remained, however. No one had yet determined what substances made up the moon's surface. And scientists argued over whether the moon's unique landforms had been shaped by meteor strikes or volcanic activity. Debates also raged over whether there was life on the moon.

The lighter-colored areas seen on images of Earth's moon are hilly regions that contain a rock called anorthosite, which is usually white.

Until the mid-1900s, it was impossible to answer these questions, as people could get no closer to the moon than a telescopic lens would allow. During World War II (1939–45), however, many countries began to research and develop rockets for use in warfare. After the war, the research continued, especially in the U.S., where German rocket scientist Wernher von Braun set out to design rockets that could reach EARTH ORBIT. At the same time, scientists in the Soviet Union worked to develop their own rockets. Soon, the two countries, already in the midst of the COLD WAR, were locked in an intense race for achievements in space, both believing that winning the "space race" would prove their country's technological superiority.

EXPEDITION JOURNAL

NEIL ARMSTRONG
July 17, 1969 (television transmission from Columbia*)*

We are very comfortable up here, though. We do have a happy home. There's plenty of room for the three of us, and I think we're all learning to find our favorite little corner to sit in. Zero G is very comfortable, but after a while you get to the point where you sort of get tired of rattling around and banging off the ceiling and the floor and the side, so you tend to find a little corner somewhere and put your knees up or something like that to wedge yourself in, and that seems more at home.

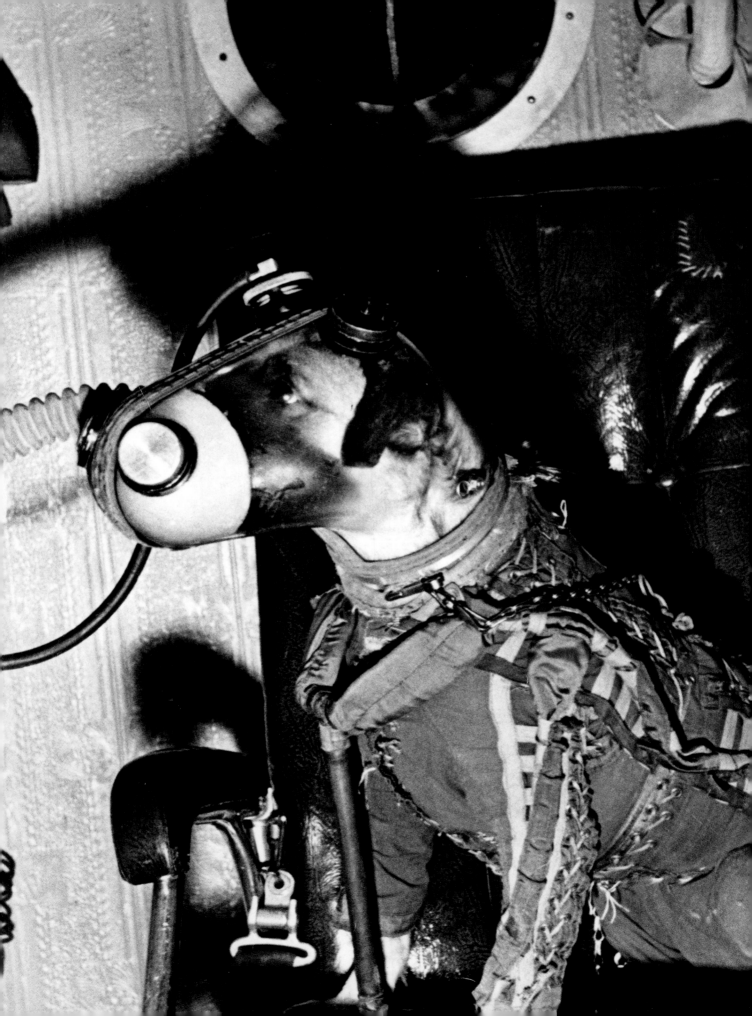

From the beginning, the Soviet Union dominated the space race, sending *Sputnik*, the world's first artificial satellite, into Earth orbit in October 1957. Only a month later, the Soviets launched *Sputnik 2*, with a dog named Laika aboard. After a failed attempt in December 1957, the Americans finally sent their first satellite into the skies on January 31, 1958. The Soviets remained in the lead, however, sending the first unmanned spacecraft around the moon in October 1959 and then launching COSMONAUT Yuri Gagarin into space in April 1961, making him both the first human in space and the first to orbit the Earth. The next month, astronaut Alan Shepard became the first American in space, but it wasn't until February 1962 that John Glenn would become the first American to orbit the planet.

Laika died within hours after Sputnik 2's launch, but her pioneering flight enabled humans such as Yuri Gagarin (above) to attempt further missions.

On September 12, 1962, at Houston's Rice University, President Kennedy famously said, "We choose to go to the moon in this decade and do the other things, not because they are easy, but because they are hard."

By then, though, America had its sights on an even loftier goal. On May 25, 1961, president John F. Kennedy had made a dramatic announcement before both houses of the U.S. Congress: "I believe that this nation should commit itself to achieving the goal, before this decade is out, of landing a man on the moon and returning him safely to the earth," he said. Since this task could cost $7 to 9 billion, Kennedy appealed to Congress to increase funding for the National Aeronautics and Space Administration (NASA), which had replaced a previous aeronautics agency in 1958.

Within months of Kennedy's announcement, NASA began to launch unmanned moon probes but was plagued by a series of failures. It wasn't until July 1964 that *Ranger 7* became the first to successfully relay information from the moon. It was followed by several additional probes, some of which photographed the moon from lunar orbit, while others landed on the surface and sent back analyses of its composition. Work on spacecraft development also continued. Already, Project Mercury's one-man space flights had shown that astronauts could survive the extreme acceleration force (G-force) placed on their bodies as they exited Earth's atmosphere

APOLLO 11 PROFILE: NEIL ARMSTRONG

Born on August 5, 1930, in Wapakoneta, Ohio, Neil

Armstrong received his pilot's license at the age of 16. He

studied aeronautical engineering at Purdue University and

later earned a master of science in aerospace engineering

from the University of Southern California. After flying

combat missions during the Korean War, Armstrong served

as a test pilot at Edwards Air Force Base in California. He

joined NASA in 1962, and in March 1966 flew on Gemini

8. After serving as commander of Apollo 11, Armstrong

became deputy associate administrator for aeronautics in

NASA's Office of Advanced Research and Technology. He

retired a year later to teach aerospace engineering at the

University of Cincinnati until 1979. In 1986, Armstrong

served on the presidential commission that investigated the

explosion of the space shuttle *Challenger*.

and that they could function in the weightlessness of space. In 1965, NASA began sending two-man crews into space as part of Project Gemini. By November 1966, 10 manned Gemini missions had successfully tested the various maneuvers—including that of docking two crafts in space—required for a manned moon landing.

NASA employees then threw themselves into the lunar landing program, named Project Apollo. Before the program had even launched its first mission, however, it was beset by tragedy. In January 1967, the three-man crew of Apollo 1 was killed when their command module (the part of the spacecraft that holds the astronauts) caught fire during a SIMULATION on the launch pad. Although it at first seemed that the fire might put an end to the Apollo program, less than two years later, in October 1968, Apollo 7 rocketed into Earth orbit, becoming the first successful manned Apollo mission. In December of that year, Apollo 8 became the first manned spacecraft to orbit the moon. In March 1969, Apollo 9 tested the lunar module (the part of the spacecraft that would land on the moon) in Earth orbit, and two months later, Apollo 10 tested it in lunar orbit, flying to within 50,000 feet (15,240 m) of the lunar surface. With the success of these "rehearsal" missions, it looked as though the next Apollo crew would be the one to land on the moon. Slated for that mission was the three-man team of Neil Armstrong, Buzz Aldrin, and Michael Collins.

The relatively unscathed exterior of Apollo 1's command module belied the inferno that had claimed the lives of Gus Grissom, Edward White, and Roger Chaffee.

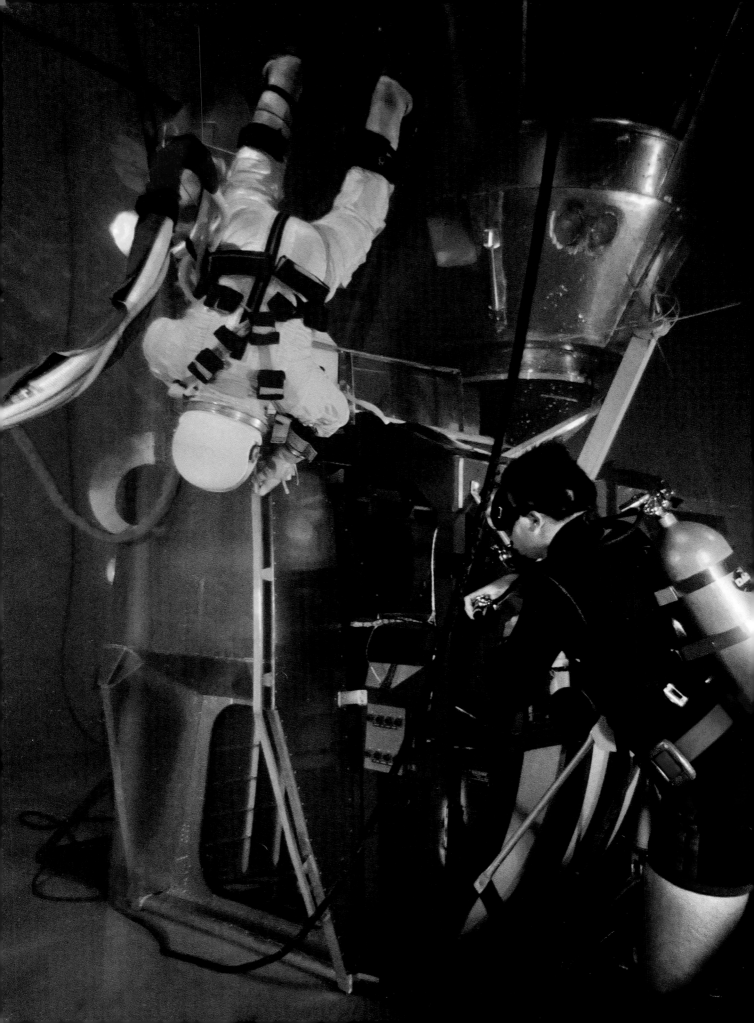

THE GREATEST ADVENTURE

Although Armstrong, Aldrin, and Collins had undergone a rigorous selection process in order to become astronauts, they were chosen for the first lunar landing mission by chance. When NASA was first established in 1958, adventurers from across the country sought to become astronauts. NASA's leaders were not looking for daredevils, though. They wanted stable 25- to 40-year-old men (there were initially no women astronauts) with a college education. The men also needed to be able to fly; thus, NASA turned to the U.S. military and its test pilots for the first candidates. Armstrong joined the ranks of the astronaut corps in 1962, and Aldrin and Collins were accepted the next year. All three astronauts traveled into space on separate Gemini missions before continuing to Project Apollo, where Deke Slayton, the director of flight crew operations, put them together as a crew, with Armstrong as commander. In choosing crews for Apollo flights, Slayton's method was to have

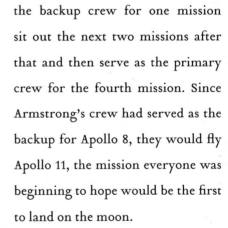

Astronauts practiced their maneuvers in the earthly environment that most closely simulated space's zero gravity— underwater.

the backup crew for one mission sit out the next two missions after that and then serve as the primary crew for the fourth mission. Since Armstrong's crew had served as the backup for Apollo 8, they would fly Apollo 11, the mission everyone was beginning to hope would be the first to land on the moon.

After learning in January 1969 that they would be flying on Apollo 11 in July, Armstrong and his crew began a period of intense training. They spent long days in simulators designed to look and act exactly like the Apollo spacecraft. Film screens and a small computer that displayed various numerical codes presented the astronauts with countless scenarios of what might go wrong during the flight, and they had to figure out how to respond to each situation. In addition to their simulator training, the astronauts took lessons in photography, astronomy, and GEOLOGY, along with spending time in a water tank that mimicked lunar gravity, which is equal to one-sixth of the force of gravity on Earth.

The CSMs used for Project Apollo were 36.2 feet (11 m) tall and weighed 66,871 pounds (30,332 kg), requiring heavy machinery to move them.

As the three men were readying themselves for their expedition, their spacecraft was also undergoing preparations. Like all Apollo spacecraft, Apollo 11 consisted of three parts: the command module (CM), the service module (SM), and the lunar module (LM). The gumdrop-shaped CM, which would be piloted by Collins, was the spacecraft's cockpit and would also serve as living quarters for the crew during the flight to the moon and back. For most of the journey, the CM would be attached to the SM, which contained the support systems, such as oxygen and fuel, that would allow the astronauts to survive in space. (Together, the CM and SM were referred to as the CSM.) The spider-shaped LM, which Aldrin would pilot, would carry him and Armstrong from lunar orbit to the surface of the moon and then back into orbit. The 3 modules of the spacecraft would sit atop a

EXPEDITION JOURNAL

WALTER CRONKITE
CBS news commentator, July 20, 1969

I was rather appalled as a supposedly professional reporter—communicator—talker—that sitting here, I really was caught speechless. I don't think that's happened in my life. Perhaps the moment when we knew that President Kennedy was dead. But this moment we were prepared for, really. We've been talking about what these fellows were going to say when they landed, and they were talking away. They had their things to report, their job to do. But I—my mouth and my throat.... As a matter of fact, Armstrong's words were as eloquent as you could ask: "Eagle has landed!" What more could you say?

281-foot-tall (86 m) Saturn V rocket. Constructed under von Braun's leadership, the rocket consisted of three separate stages that would detach from the craft at various points during the mission in order to reduce its weight.

Apollo 11's Saturn V rocket made the three-mile (5 km) journey to the launch pad on the crawler via a special route called the "Crawlerway."

All of these components were constructed by corporations across America—12,000 of them, in fact, including North American Aviation and the Boeing Company. In all, more than 400,000 people helped build Apollo 11. As each part of the spacecraft was completed, it was transferred to the 525-foot-tall (160 m) Vehicle Assembly Building at NASA's Kennedy Space Center off the eastern coast of central Florida. There the components were put together and subjected to 587,500 inspections and tests that covered such phenomena as fire, ice, collision, and dust. By May 1969, the fully assembled Apollo 11 was painstakingly transferred to its launch pad aboard a 3,000-ton (2,722 t) machine called a crawler that could move at a top speed of 1 mile (1.6 km) per hour. Then Apollo 11 underwent yet more tests and inspections as launch day—July 16—approached. In choosing the date and time of liftoff, NASA had taken into account weather forecasts, available daylight at the launch and recovery sites, and the path of the moon's orbit (which varies between 221,000 and 252,586 miles, or 355,665–406,498 km, from Earth).

Finally, the day arrived. Just over 2 hours before the scheduled launch at 9:32 A.M. eastern standard time, Armstrong, Aldrin, and Collins entered an elevator in the launch tower, which took them up 36 stories to the hatch of the CSM, named *Columbia*. (Apollo 11's LM was dubbed *Eagle*). Enclosed in their protective spacesuits, the men

were strapped firmly onto their reclined acceleration couches, which had been custom-made to fit each astronaut's body and cushion him from the force of liftoff and reentry. The astronauts were packed close together in the cramped space, which was only 11 feet (3.4 m) high and 13 feet (4 m) across at its widest point. Above them, *Columbia*'s massive dashboard was covered with more than 400 switches and controls. These would allow the men to monitor and operate the spacecraft with the assistance of two small computers, each less powerful than a modern cell phone. Scattered in open spaces throughout the CM were storage compartments for holding toothbrushes, food, and medical equipment. There were also star charts and navigational tools such as a SEXTANT. Fastened at *Columbia*'s tip was a launch escape tower, which would pull the craft free from Apollo 11's rockets and land it in the Atlantic Ocean should anything go wrong during the launch.

At nine seconds before liftoff, the five powerful engines that made up the first stage of the Saturn V rocket ignited, sending a roaring fireball into a water-filled pit beneath the rocket. As the engines built up to full power, the clamps holding Apollo 11 to the launch tower were released, and it began to rise slowly into the air. Gradually, the rocket picked up speed, clearing the launch tower 12 seconds after liftoff. Its deafening roar drowned out the screams of "Go! Go!" by the more than 1 million spectators who had crowded into central Florida to watch the history-making launch. The Parisian newspaper *Le Figaro* summed up the feelings of people around the world that morning by proclaiming, "The greatest adventure in the history of humanity has begun."

APOLLO 11 PROFILE: BUZZ ALDRIN

Edwin "Buzz" Aldrin was born on January 20, 1930,

in Montclair, New Jersey. He graduated from the U.S.

Military Academy at West Point and flew fighter jets during

the Korean War before earning a doctor of science in

astronautics from MIT. Aldrin joined NASA in 1963, and

in November 1966, he flew on Gemini 12. After serving as

LM pilot for Apollo 11, Aldrin worked with NASA on the

shuttle program before retiring in 1971. He later struggled

with depression and alcoholism, which he wrote about

in his memoirs *Return to Earth* (1973) and *Magnificent

Desolation: The Long Journey Home from the Moon* (2009).

Aldrin has also written a number of other books, both fiction

and nonfiction. Today, he dedicates much of his time to

promoting the development of affordable space travel for all.

As the rocket boosters ignited and Apollo 11 began launching, the gantry (a bridgelike structure used for servicing the rocket) gradually disconnected, allowing the Saturn V to accelerate.

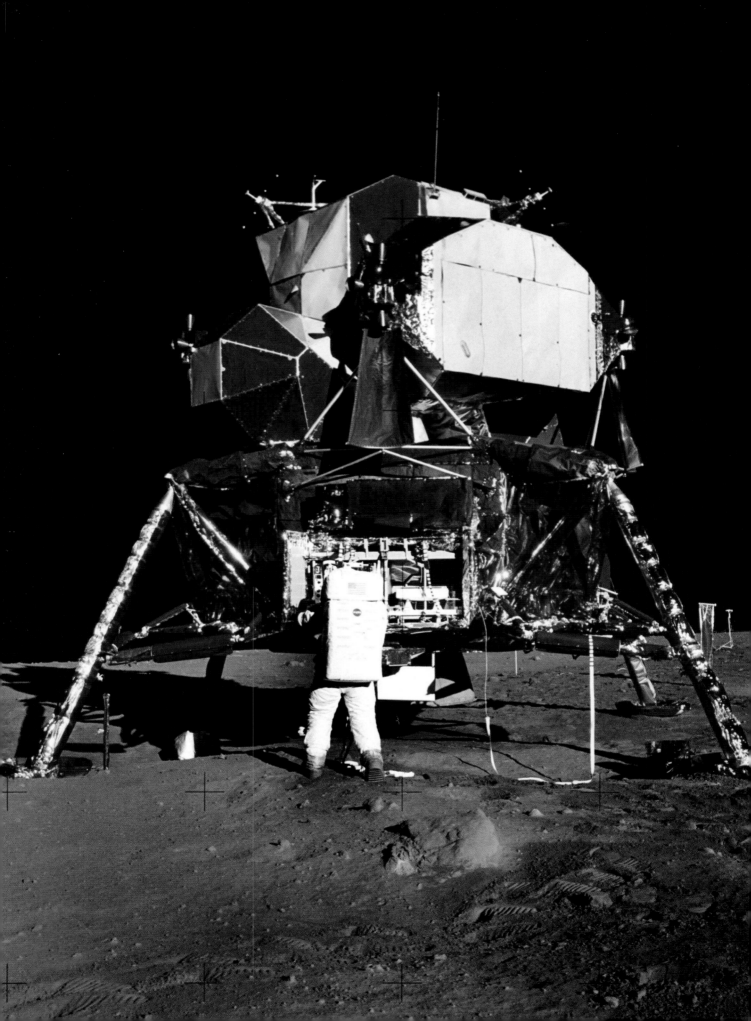

An *Eagle* Lands

As Apollo 11 began its ascent into the heavens, the astronauts inside were shaken back and forth in their seats. The more the rocket accelerated, the greater the G-force became, reaching 4.5 G about a minute into the flight, which made each astronaut feel a crushing pressure equal to 4.5 times his normal body weight.

Two minutes and 40 seconds after liftoff, Apollo 11 was 41 miles (66 km) above Earth's surface, traveling at 6,100 miles (9,817 km) per hour. Its 4.5 million pounds (2 million kg) of fuel spent, the first stage of the Saturn V separated from the rest of the craft and fell into the Atlantic. Next, the Saturn V's second stage fired its 5 engines, which powered the rocket to a speed of 15,500 miles (25,000 km) per hour. After burning for six minutes, this stage shut down and disengaged, plunging into the ocean below. Now that the dangerous part of launching was over, the launch escape tower also fell away from the craft, enabling the astronauts to see the blackness outside their windows.

The tools the astronauts needed for exploring the lunar surface were located in the LM's Modularized Equipment Stowage Assembly.

Apollo 11 was now 115 miles (185 km) above the earth, and the Saturn V's third stage briefly fired its single engine to stabilize the craft in Earth orbit. Once in orbit, the astronauts completed a final check of their spacecraft before again firing their third-stage engine, accelerating the craft to a speed of 24,182 miles (38,917 km) per hour and breaking it out of Earth orbit. Then the LM's protective "garage" on the third stage of the Saturn V was opened, and Collins maneuvered a probe on the CSM into a hole on the LM to attach the two modules before releasing the third stage into orbit around the sun.

Once their spacecraft was well on its way to

the moon, the astronauts could finally take off their spacesuits and helmets. With their restraints removed, they could float freely around the cabin, taking advantage of the lack of gravity. Although Apollo 11 was hurtling through space at a rate of six miles (9.7 km) per second, the crew did not feel as if the craft was moving at all.

The astronauts had plenty to do during the flight. Collins was responsible for keeping *Columbia* in good condition, with tasks such as replacing the filters that removed carbon dioxide from the air and emptying the fuel cells of impurities that could build up and drain electrical power. Armstrong and Aldrin spent much of their time studying photographs of the moon's surface to prepare for the lunar landing. The crew remained in constant radio contact with MISSION CONTROL, based at the Manned Spacecraft Center in Houston, Texas, and led by flight director Gene Kranz. They also filmed a number of television broadcasts during the course of the flight, allowing people around the world to get a firsthand glimpse of their journey.

When the astronauts got hungry, they could choose from freeze-dried foods such as roast beef, ham, potatoes, bacon, and applesauce. To eat these entrees, the astronauts first squirted hot water into the vacuum-sealed bags and then kneaded the bags until their contents were thick and mushy, like toothpaste. Dried pears, peaches, bacon bits, and peanut cubes were also available. During rest periods, the astronauts climbed into lightweight sleeping bags and tied themselves down to keep from bumping into one another—or into the craft's many switches.

Finally, after coasting through more than 200,000 miles (321,870 km) of space in 75 hours, Apollo 11 reached the moon on July 19.

EXPEDITION JOURNAL

Neil Armstrong
July 20, 1969 (television transmission from the moon)

The surface is fine and powdery. I can—I can pick it up loosely with my toe. It does adhere in fine layers like powdered charcoal to the sole and sides of my boots. I only go in a small fraction of an inch, maybe an eighth of an inch, but I can see the footprints of my boots and the treads in the fine, sandy particles. There seems to be no difficulty in moving around as we suspected. It's even perhaps easier than the simulations at one-sixth G that we performed in the simulations on the ground. It's actually no trouble to walk around.

Collins slowed the spacecraft so that it would fall into lunar orbit 69 miles (111 km) above the moon's surface. The next day, after having orbited the moon almost 13 times in 25 hours, Armstrong and Aldrin wrangled into their spacesuits and entered the *Eagle*. When they were ready, Collins pushed a button, releasing the LM from the CSM and sending his crewmates on their way to the moon, while he remained in orbit.

One hundred hours and 39 minutes into the mission, the LM was released from the CSM and Aldrin and Armstrong began their descent to the surface.

Inside the *Eagle*, Armstrong and Aldrin stood side-by-side, their shoes strapped to the floor and their waists tied to the walls. Only slightly larger than the CM, the LM's cabin was crowded with circuit breakers, wires, pipes, and even part of the ascent engine, so Armstrong and Aldrin were left with only about four feet (1.2 m) in which to maneuver. In front of them, the LM's large instrument panel was flanked by two small, triangle-shaped windows.

Guided by its computer, the *Eagle* began its descent. Suddenly, just over 33,000 feet (10,058 m) from the surface, the computer began issuing alarms that neither Armstrong nor Aldrin had encountered during training. Although they feared the alarms might force them to abort, or quit, mission control determined that the computer was overloaded but would continue to perform. *Eagle* was "go" to continue.

Due to the commotion raised by the alarms, Armstrong and Aldrin had not been able to look out their window during much of the descent. When Armstrong, who was at the controls, finally ventured a peek, he discovered that the computer's autopilot, which had been

preprogrammed to land the craft, was going to overshoot the planned landing site. The problem arose because the *Eagle* was flying faster than expected. Realizing that if the *Eagle* remained on autopilot, it would land in a field strewn with boulders as large as cars, Armstrong took over control from the computer to manually fly the craft. As he scanned the ground for a safe landing spot, the LM's fuel warning alarm came on, meaning the craft had only 90 seconds of fuel left. Armstrong had to either land or abort before the fuel ran out, as an absence of fuel would send the *Eagle* crashing to the surface. As the flight controllers in Houston—who had no way of seeing or detecting the lunar boulders—nervously watched the *Eagle's* fuel levels fall, Armstrong finally found the place he was looking for. The craft touched down so lightly that neither man felt it, but Aldrin saw the instrument panel's "contact" light glow, indicating that one of the LM's sensors had touched the surface. The astronauts shut the engine down with only 17 seconds of fuel remaining. Then Armstrong radioed mission control: "Houston, Tranquility Base here. The *Eagle* has landed."

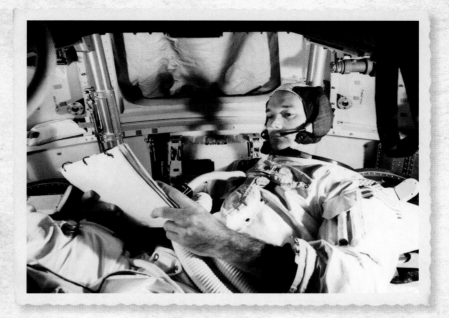

APOLLO 11 PROFILE: MICHAEL COLLINS

The son of a U.S. Army officer, Michael Collins was born on

October 31, 1930, in Rome, Italy, and spent his childhood in

various U.S. cities, including Baltimore and San Antonio.

Collins graduated from the U.S. Military Academy at West

Point before becoming a test pilot at Edwards Air Force Base.

He joined the astronaut corps in 1963 and in July 1966 flew on

Gemini 10. After piloting the CSM during Apollo 11, Collins

retired from NASA to serve as assistant secretary of state

for public affairs before becoming the first director of the

Smithsonian's National Air and Space Museum. Collins has

written a number of books, including *Carrying the Fire:*

An Astronaut's Journeys (1974), about his experience on

Apollo 11.

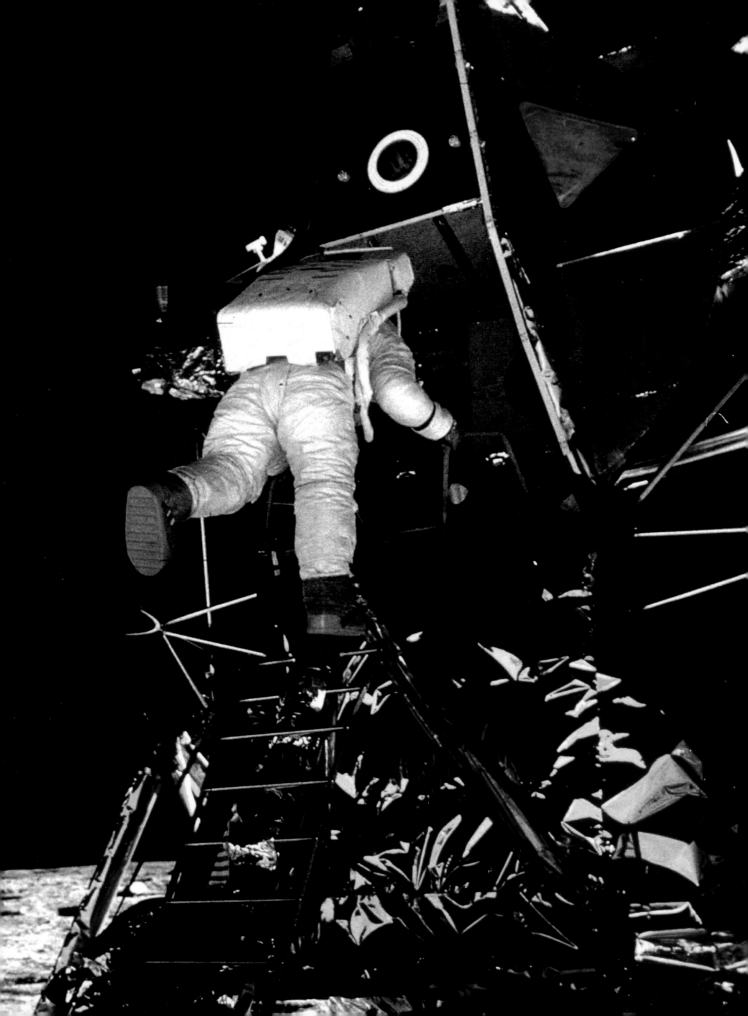

One Small Step

AFTER THE *Eagle* LANDED, ARMSTRONG AND ALDRIN TOOK A MOMENT TO SHAKE HANDS. THEN THEY TURNED THEIR ATTENTION TO THE CRAFT'S INSTRUMENT PANEL, TAKING READINGS AND TESTING SYSTEMS TO ENSURE THAT THE LM WAS READY TO MAKE AN EMERGENCY LIFTOFF, SHOULD THAT BECOME NECESSARY. TWO HOURS LATER, AFTER RUNNING DOWN AN

extensive to-do list, Armstrong and Aldrin began to prepare to take their first steps on the moon. Each man strapped on a portable life support system (PLSS), a backpack that contained the oxygen he would need to breathe as well as his radio connection to Earth and a water circulation system to cool the long johns worn underneath the spacesuit. The spacesuits themselves—made of 25 layers of nylon, Teflon, neoprene, Mylar, and other materials—would operate as mini-spaceships, protecting the men from the moon's many potential dangers. Without the suits, the moon's extreme temperatures (ranging from -250 °F, or -157 °C, in the shade to 225 °F, or 107 °C, in the sun), lack

As Aldrin exited the LM, Armstrong documented it on film and also took pictures of the module itself, to show how it had held up during landing.

of air, solar radiation, or MICRO-METEORITES could have killed the men almost instantly. After spending three hours donning their suits, along with protective helmets, boots, and gloves, Armstrong and Aldrin were at last ready to exit the LM.

Armstrong was first. He opened the *Eagle's* hatch and slowly made his way down its ladder, pulling a ring to release a television camera as he did so. A human's first step on the moon would be witnessed by more than 600 million people on Earth. As he stepped off the ladder's last rung, Armstrong famously said, "That's one small step for [a] man, one giant leap for mankind." When Aldrin exited the *Eagle* 14 minutes later, he characterized

Shortly after planting the flag on the moon, Armstrong and Aldrin spoke with president Richard Nixon through a telephone-radio transmission.

what he saw as "magnificent desolation."

The LM had landed on the southern edge of the Sea of Tranquility, a large plain dotted with craters and boulders. Although the surface had looked forbidding when viewed from lunar orbit, up close it was much less intimidating, its color ranging from light tan to gray, depending on the angle of the sun. Although the sun's glare made it impossible to see stars in the blackness of outer space, the men could clearly see the blue dot of Earth—looking smaller than a golf ball—in the distance. For just over two hours, Armstrong and Aldrin bounced across the moon's surface, enjoying the feeling of weighing only one-sixth as much as they did on Earth. During that time, they took photographs,

EXPEDITION JOURNAL

Michael Collins
July 23, 1969 (television transmission from Columbia)

This trip of ours to the moon may have looked, to you, simple or easy. I'd like to say that it has not been a game.... We have always had confidence that all this equipment will work, and work properly, and we continue to have confidence that it will do so for the remainder of the flight. All this is possible only through the blood, sweat, and tears of a number of people. First, the American workmen who put these pieces of machinery together in the factory. Second, the painstaking work done by the various test teams.... And finally, the people at the Manned Spacecraft Center, both in management, in mission planning, in flight control, and last, but not least, in crew training. This operation is somewhat like the periscope of a submarine. All you see is the three of us, but beneath the surface are thousands and thousands of others, and to all those, I would like to say, thank you very much.

collected rock samples, erected an American flag, and set out SEISMOMETERS and other scientific equipment.

After their moonwalk, Armstrong and Aldrin returned to the *Eagle* to rest and prepare to leave. When they lifted off from the surface on July 21, firing a separate engine used only for ascent, they left behind the landing stage, or bottom half, of the LM. On one of its legs was a plaque reading, "Here men from the planet Earth first set foot upon the moon. July 1969 A.D. We came in peace for all mankind."

The *Eagle* was soon reunited with *Columbia* and Collins. After the two craft had docked and Armstrong and Aldrin had reentered the CSM, *Eagle* was jettisoned. Then Collins fired *Columbia*'s engine to break out of lunar orbit, and the men were on their way back to Earth. Two and a half days later, just before reentering the atmosphere, they released the SM, leaving only the CM to fall to Earth. After a fiery reentry, during which the men experienced a G-force of 6.3 and the temperature outside the craft rose to 5,000 °F (2,760 °C), the *Columbia* splashed into the Pacific Ocean, about 900 miles (1,448 km) southwest of Hawaii.

After the astronauts were removed and flown by helicopter to the Hornet, *the CM was retrieved from the water and placed on deck.*

The three astronauts were taken aboard the U.S. Navy aircraft carrier USS *Hornet* and immediately placed in a QUARANTINE trailer to ensure that no "moon germs" had made the journey back to Earth with them. They were transported in the trailer back to Houston, where they continued their quarantine in the more spacious Lunar Receiving Laboratory. Two weeks later, after no moon germs had been discovered, the men were cleared to leave.

Across America and around the world, Armstrong, Aldrin, and Collins were regarded as heroes, and their stunning feat was seen as proof of America's scientific and military superiority. Leaders from more than 100 foreign nations sent their congratulations. In order to capitalize on the goodwill generated by the successful moon mission, the Apollo 11 astronauts were sent on a 38-day diplomatic tour of 23 countries, including England, Japan, Iran, and Spain. Upon their return, Collins took a position with the U.S. state department, while Armstrong and Aldrin remained with NASA for a time, although neither ever returned to space.

In the years following Apollo 11's successful moon landing, six more Apollo

Aldrin, Collins, and Armstrong (from left to right, waving in lead car) were treated to a ticker-tape parade in New York City on August 13, 1969.